WORLD HERITAGE

Protecting Threatened Animals

Brendan and Debbie Gallagher

A⁺

Clifton Park - Halfmoon Public Library
475 Moe Road
Clifton Park, New York 12065

This edition first published in 2011 in the United States of America by Smart Apple Media. All rights reserved. No part of this book may be reproduced in any form or by any means without written permission from the publisher.

Smart Apple Media
P.O. Box 3263
Mankato, MN, 56002

First published in 2010 by
MACMILLAN EDUCATION AUSTRALIA PTY LTD
15–19 Claremont St, South Yarra, Australia 3141

Visit our web site at www.macmillan.com.au or go directly to www.macmillanlibrary.com.au

Associated companies and representatives throughout the world.

Copyright © Brendan and Debbie Gallagher 2010

Library of Congress Cataloging-in-Publication Data

Gallagher, Brendan.
    Protecting threatened animals / Brendan and Debbie Gallagher.
        p. cm. — (World heritage)
    Includes index.
    ISBN 978-1-59920-582-3 (library bound)
    1. Endangered species—Juvenile literature. 2. Wildlife conservation—Juvenile literature. I. Gallagher, Debbie, 1969– II. Title.
    QL83.G35 2011
    591.68—dc22
                                                    2009053020

5758

Publisher: Carmel Heron
Managing Editor: Vanessa Lanaway
Editor: Kirstie Innes-Will
Proofreader: Paige Amor
Designer: Kerri Wilson
Page layout: Kerri Wilson
Photo researcher: Legend Images
Illustrator: Guy Holt
Production Controller: Vanessa Johnson

Manufactured in China by Macmillan Production (Asia) Ltd.
Kwun Tong, Kowloon, Hong Kong
Supplier Code: CP December 2009

Acknowledgments
Cover photograph of Javan Rhinoceros, Indonesia courtesy of Photolibrary/OSF/Mary Plage

Photographs courtesy of:
© Jean-Paul Ferrero/Auscape, 20; Luis Cardona, 17; © Tom Brakefield/Corbis, 8; © Frans Lanting/Corbis, 12, 15; © Kevin Schafer/Corbis, 16; Daniel J Cox/Getty Images, 10; DEA/P. Jaccod/Getty Images, 18; Jason Edwards/Getty Images, 6; Tim Laman/Getty Images, 13; Adam Pretty/Getty Images, 27; Art Wolfe/Getty Images, 14; Photolibrary/Eric Baccega, 23; Photolibrary/Tom Brakefield, 26; Photolibrary/Juan Carlos Munoz, 31; Photolibrary/OSF/Mary Plage, 1, 30; Photolibrary/Yan Hong Huang/Redlink, 22; Photolibrary/Mark Stouffer, 9; Roland Seitre, 24; © Pichugin Dmitry/Shutterstock, 7; © Jonathan G/ Shutterstock, 11; © Song Heming/Shutterstock, 19; © Rachael Russell/Shutterstock, 29; © YoavPeled/Shutterstock, 28; © Tian Zhan/Shutterstock, 25; Colleen Sims, W.A. Dept of Environment and Conservation (DEC), 21.
Fact File IUCN Red List Status throughout is courtesy of IUCN 2009. IUCN Red List of Threatened Species. Version 2009.1. <www.iucnredlist.org>. Downloaded on 04 October 2009

Please note
At the time of printing, the Internet addresses appearing in this book were correct. Owing to the dynamic nature of the Internet, however, we cannot guarantee that all these addresses will remain correct.

Contents

When a word in the text is printed in **bold**, look for its meaning in the glossary boxes.

World Heritage

There are places around the world that are important to all peoples. We call these places the world's heritage. Some of these places are human creations, such as the pyramids of Egypt. Some are natural creations, such as the Great Barrier Reef of Australia.

The World Heritage List

The World Heritage List is a list of **sites** that must be protected because they have some kind of outstanding importance for the world. This list was created in 1972, and new places are added every year. Each site on the World Heritage List belongs to one of the following categories:

 NATURAL – for example, waterfalls, forests, or deserts

CULTURAL – for example, a building or a site where an event occurred

MIXED – if it has both natural and cultural features

UNESCO

UNESCO, the United Nations Educational, Scientific, and Cultural Organization, is the organization that maintains the World Heritage List. Find out more at www.unesco.org.

World Heritage Criteria

A place can be **inscribed** on the World Heritage List if it meets at least one of these ten **criteria** and is an outstanding example of it. The criteria are:

 i a masterpiece of human creative genius

ii a site representing the sharing of human ideas

 iii a site representing a special culture or civilization

 iv a historical building or landscape from a period of history

 v a site representing or important to a traditional culture

 vi a site representing an important event, idea, living tradition, or belief

vii a very beautiful or unique natural site

viii a site showing evidence of Earth's history

ix an important ecosystem

x an important natural habitat for species protection

KEY TERMS

sites	places
inscribed	added to
criteria	rules or requirements

Protecting Threatened Animals

Protecting Threatened Animals is about protecting rare and threatened **species**. To protect an animal, its **habitat** must also be protected. When some animals are not protected, they may be in danger of becoming **extinct**. The International Union for the Conservation of Nature (IUCN) has made a list called the Red List, which describes the level of danger facing animal species. On the IUCN Red List animals facing a high risk of **extinction** are described as *vulnerable*. Animals facing a very high risk of extinction are described as *endangered*. Animals facing an extremely high risk of extinction are described as *critically endangered*.

Criteria for Protecting Threatened Animals

Many of the places featured in this book are important for several reasons. This book focuses on just one reason: how a natural habitat protects one or more endangered animal species. This is reason x on the list of reasons for being on the World Heritage List.

Protecting World Heritage

Governments around the world have all agreed to protect the sites on the World Heritage List. A site that is not being properly looked after may be put on the List of World Heritage in Danger. See http://whc.unesco.org/en/158/

This map shows the location of the World Heritage sites covered in this book.

Caption

N

Arctic Circle

NORTH AMERICA

EUROPE

ASIA

Central Sikhote-Alin

Tropic of Cancer

Everglades National Park

Sichuan Giant Panda Sanctuaries

Royal Chitwan National Park

The Sundarbans

Río Plátano Biosphere Reserve

AFRICA

Equator

Galápagos Islands

SOUTH AMERICA

Bwindi Impenetrable National Park

Ujung Kulon National Park

Tropic of Capricorn

Iguaçu National Park

Shark Bay, Western Australia

AUSTRALIA

Tasmanian Wilderness

Te Wahipounamu

species	groups of plants or animals that have something in common
habitat	a place where animals or plants live or grow
extinct	completely dead, no longer having any living examples
extinction	dying out, complete destruction of a species

Bwindi Impenetrable National Park

Bwindi Impenetrable National Park in Uganda is a forest on steep mountains. It is called **impenetrable** because it has a thick **understory** of vines and shrubs. Many endangered species are found in the park, including the mountain gorilla.

FACT FILE

UGANDA

Bwindi protects nearly 300 mountain gorillas, about half of the world's wild population.

IUCN Red List status of mountain gorilla: endangered

Category:

Criteria:

The endangered mountain gorillas in Bwindi eat leaves, bark stems, and fruit. At night they make a bed of plants to sleep on.

vines

trees

bark

mountain gorilla

TIMELINE

1932
Bwindi is made a forest reserve.

1961
Bwindi becomes an animal sanctuary to protect the mountain gorillas.

1991
The sanctuary is made a national park.

1994
The site is inscribed on the World Heritage List.

Farms are developed up to the edge of the park, but its World Heritage status protects against further development.

Important Features

Mountain gorillas are the largest of the **primates**, and can grow to over 5 feet (1.5 meters) in height. They live at very high **altitudes** in thick forests. Bwindi has the richest variety of tree and fern species in east Africa, and 60 percent of the forest has an altitude of 6,562 feet (2,000 meters) or more, so it makes a good home for the gorillas. The many different trees and ferns provide the mountain gorillas with food.

Did You Know?

Bwindi National Park is the only remaining place in the world where both chimpanzees and mountain gorillas live.

Issues

Bwindi used to be part of a much larger forest, but the unprotected parts have been completely cut down, leaving Bwindi as an island of forest surrounded by farms. Protecting the remaining habitat is important for the survival of the gorillas.

GLOSSARY

impenetrable	impossible to get through
understory	the area beneath the trees of a forest
primates	the group of mammals that includes monkeys and humans
altitudes	heights above sea level

Central Sikhote-Alin

Central Sikhote-Alin, in the Russian Federation, is a **temperate forest**. It is one of the most **diverse** temperate forests in the world. Similar habitats have been destroyed, and Central Sikhote-Alin is the last of its type. Central Sikhote-Alin protects the Amur tiger, also known as the Siberian tiger.

FACT FILE

RUSSIAN FEDERATION

Central Sikhote-Alin protects about 90 percent of the 450 wild Amur tigers left in the world.

IUCN Red List status of Amur tiger: endangered

Category:

Criteria:

Amur tiger

snow cover in winter

The endangered Amur tiger of Sikhote-Alin grows a thick winter coat to survive in the cold winters of Central Sikhote-Alin.

TIMELINE

1930
There are only 30 to 40 wild Amur tigers alive.

1935
Sikhote-Alin is made a nature reserve.

1947
Russia becomes the first country to give its tigers full protection.

2001
Central Sikhote-Alin is inscribed on the World Heritage List.

2005
Between 331 and 393 tigers that are more than 20 months old live in Central Sikhote-Alin.

Important Features

Amur tigers are usually **solitary** animals. Each tiger has its own area, with male and female areas overlapping. Sikhote-Alin is big enough that each tiger has an area of about 174 square miles (450 square kilometers). They need a wide availability of food, especially wild pigs and deer, as each Amur tiger kills about about 50 large animals per year.

Issues

Tigers were once spread throughout Asia, but because of hunting, **poaching**, and the loss of their habitat, they are now found in only 7 percent of the land they once used to occupy. Poaching continues to be a major problem, as tiger body parts are used in traditional Asian medicines.

This tiger is caught in a foot trap set by a poacher. Poaching is a major problem in Sikhote-Alin.

GLOSSARY

temperate forest	a forest with a mild climate
diverse	having a wide variety
solitary	living alone
poaching	the hunting of animals where it is not allowed

Everglades National Park

Everglades National Park is an area of **marshlands** in the southeast of the United States. Within the park's wetlands there are also drier parts, such as forests of **conifers** and tree islands, called *hammocks*. The conifer forests and hammocks are vital to the protection of many endangered species, including the Florida panther.

In the drier areas of the Everglades, the critically endangered Florida panthers often prey on hogs and deer but they will also eat raccoons and armadillos.

conifer forest

freshwater river

Florida panther

forest

TIMELINE

1934	1979	1993	1995	2007
The Everglades are made a national park.	The site is inscribed on the World Heritage List.	The park is added to the List of World Heritage in Danger.	There are only 20 to 30 panthers in the park. Eight female panthers are introduced to increase the population.	The park is removed from the List of World Heritage in Danger.

Important Features

The Florida panther is a **solitary** animal, with each panther living in a large area. On average, male panthers have a home range of more than 8 square miles (20 square kilometers). These ranges cross into the home ranges of female panthers. Both male and female panthers do best in the drier areas of their ranges, like the hammocks of the Everglades. There, they can prey on deer and hogs.

Issues

Unprotected areas around the Everglades include roads which break up the panther's habitat. In 2008, at least ten panthers were killed in collisions with cars. Underground passes have helped to prevent panther deaths. The site was placed on the List of World Heritage in Danger due to damage from pollution and hurricanes, among other things, but government actions addressed these issues.

Did You Know?
The Florida panther is one of the most endangered mammals on Earth.

Road signs in the area warn about panthers crossing the roads, as many panthers die this way.

GLOSSARY

marshlands	flooded grassy plains
conifers	trees or shrubs like pine trees that grow seeds on cones
solitary	living alone

Galápagos Islands

The 120 Galápagos Islands belong to Ecuador. There are hundreds of threatened species on the islands, including the Galápagos giant tortoise, from which the islands take their name.

FACT FILE

ECUADOR

The Galápagos Islands protect the Galápagos giant tortoise, one of 35 reptile species **endemic to the islands.**

IUCN Red List status of Galápagos giant tortoise: vulnerable

Category:

Criteria:

The vulnerable Galápagos giant tortoises are endemic to the Galápagos Islands. They sleep in muddy ponds to protect them from insects and to stay cool.

freshwater pond

Galápagos giant tortoises

TIMELINE

1900s	1936	1970s	1978	2007
Whaling and seal-hunting ships reduce tortoise numbers.	The Galápagos National Park is established.	Breeding programs begin to restore tortoise populations.	The site is inscribed on the World Heritage List.	The site is added to the List of World Heritage in Danger.

Important Features

Galápagos giant tortoises are slow-moving reptiles that live on land. Sometimes when a giant tortoise sees a Darwin's finch or a mockingbird, it stands up tall on its legs and raises its neck toward the sky, allowing the bird to pick annoying insects off its skin.

Issues

During the 1900s, people on **whaling** and seal hunting ships killed tortoises for food or to make oil. More recently, **introduced species** such as cats, pigs, and rats prey on young tortoises and tortoise eggs. This is one of many problems that led to the site being added to the List of World Heritage in Danger. **Conservationists** remove tortoise eggs from nests and breed them away from these threats.

When a tortoise's shell is at least 8 inches (20 centimeters) wide, the conservationists return the tortoise to the wild because it is big enough to fend for itself.

GLOSSARY

endemic to	only found in
whaling	the hunting of whales
introduced species	plants or animals that are not native to an area
conservationists	people who protect an area

Iguaçu National Park

Iguaçu National Park in Brazil has a mixture of **rain forest** and **deciduous forests**. Most of the original rain forest has been cut down, leaving Iguaçu as an island of forest and an important habitat for many endangered species, including the giant otter.

FACT FILE

BRAZIL

Iguaçu National Park protects the giant otter.

IUCN Red List status of giant otter: endangered

Category:

Criteria:

rain forest

giant otters

river

Iguaçu National Park is one of the few places where giant otters remain in the wild.

TIMELINE

1939	1986	1999	2001
Iguaçu is made a national park.	The site is inscribed on the World Heritage List.	The site is placed on the List of World Heritage in Danger, and the giant otter is listed as endangered.	The site is removed from the List of World Heritage in Danger.

Important Features

Giant otters are the largest of the otter species. Male giant otters can grow to 6 feet (1.8 meters) long – the average height of a human adult. They live in wetland habitats, beside gentle rivers, streams, and swamps, where fish are plentiful. They prefer areas that have a thick **understory**, where they can dig burrows under fallen logs. Giant otters mostly eat fish but will also eat small snakes and small **caiman**.

Issues

In 1997, 800 people moved into the park to reopen an old road. This encouraged **poaching** and **deforestation** because it made access to the park easier. Otters are hunted for their fur, and deforestation reduces their habitat. The park was on the List of World Heritage in Danger from 1999 to 2001, but the Brazilian government addressed this by closing the road and planting 25,000 seedlings in the disturbed areas.

> **Did You Know?**
> The giant otter has nine different calls, though their purposes are not fully understood.

Rain forest outside the park area has been cleared for farms.

GLOSSARY

rain forest	forests that receive a lot of rainfall
deciduous forests	forests of trees that lose their leaves once a year
understory	the area beneath the trees of a forest
caiman	reptiles related to crocodiles and alligators
poaching	the hunting of animals where it is not allowed
deforestation	the cutting down and removal of trees

Río Plátano Biosphere Reserve

Río Plátano **Biosphere Reserve** in Honduras is an area of **rain forest** on steep mountains. The reserve is very **diverse** and it protects many endangered species, including the Central American tapir.

FACT FILE

HONDURAS

SOUTH AMERICA

The Río Plátano Biosphere Reserve protects the Central American tapir.

IUCN Red List status of Central American tapir: endangered

Category:

Criteria:

The rare Central American tapir lives in Río Plátino. Young tapirs are a red brown colour with white stripes.

Central American tapir

young tapir

TIMELINE

1960	1969	1982	1986	2007
Río Plátano is made a reserve.	Río Plátano reserve becomes a national park.	The site is inscribed on the World Heritage List.	The site is placed on the List of World Heritage in Danger.	The site is removed from the List of World Heritage in Danger.

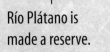

Important Features

The Central American tapir lives in thick rain forest close to swamps and **marshlands**. It is a large mammal and can grow over 3 feet (1 meter) in height and up to 6 feet (2 m) in length.

Issues

The reserve was placed on the List of World Heritage in Danger in 1986 because of **deforestation** and **poaching**. A road was also built into the park. These activities were **fragmenting** the habitat of many species, including the Central American tapir. Loss of habitat is the greatest threat to the tapir. Despite the Honduran government promising in 2007 to prevent illegal logging, deforestation has continued. The site may once again be placed on the List of World Heritage in Danger.

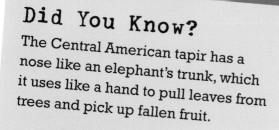

Did You Know?
The Central American tapir has a nose like an elephant's trunk, which it uses like a hand to pull leaves from trees and pick up fallen fruit.

Illegal logging continues in the Río Plátano Biosphere Reserve, one of the last areas of tropical rain forest in Central America.

GLOSSARY

biosphere reserve	an ecosystem that people can use parts of without damaging it	**marshlands**	flooded grassy plains
		deforestation	the cutting down and removal of trees
rain forest	forests that receive a lot of rainfall	**poaching**	the hunting of animals where it is not allowed
diverse	having a wide variety	**fragmenting**	breaking up

Royal Chitwan National Park

Royal Chitwan National Park is an area of forest, tall grasses, and rivers at the foot of the Himalayas, in Nepal. Chitwan is the last habitat of its type, and protects many endangered species, including the gharial, a rare **caiman** similar to a crocodile.

FACT FILE

Royal Chitwan National Park protects about 35 gharials.

IUCN Red List status of gharial: critically endangered

Category:

Criteria:

The critically endangered gharials leave the waters of the Royal Chitwan to lay eggs or to get heat from the sun.

mudflats

gharial

deep, slow-moving river

TIMELINE

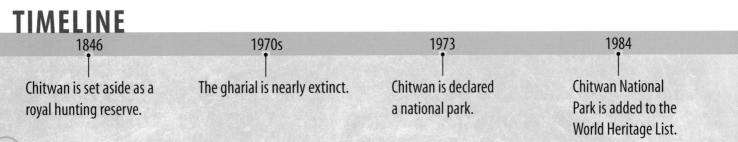

1846
Chitwan is set aside as a royal hunting reserve.

1970s
The gharial is nearly extinct.

1973
Chitwan is declared a national park.

1984
Chitwan National Park is added to the World Heritage List.

Important Features

The park provides protection for about 49 reptile species, including the critically endangered gharial. Gharials are well adapted to the rivers of Royal Chitwan, where they can find their preferred habitat of deep and slow-moving sections of rivers. Unlike crocodiles and alligators, gharials do not have strong enough jaws to eat large mammals, but they can snap very quickly to catch fish.

Issues

The main threat to gharials at Royal Chitwan comes from human activities. Fishing reduces the numbers of the fish gharials eat. Because the gharials lay their eggs in the same place each year, local people, who consider the eggs a food delicacy, take the eggs. The nesting sites need to be better protected. **Conservationists** sometimes remove eggs and raise the young gharials in captivity until they are large enough to be released back into the wild.

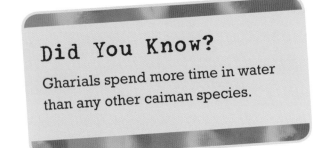

Did You Know?

Gharials spend more time in water than any other caiman species.

Human activities at Chitwan are being monitored to ensure that they do not destroy the gharial habitat.

GLOSSARY

caiman	a reptile related to crocodiles and alligators
conservationists	people who protect an area

Shark Bay, Western Australia

Shark Bay is a shallow bay with vast **sea grass** beds, islands, and peninsulas in the west of Australia. Of Australia's 26 endangered mammals, five are found on the islands of Bernier and Dorre in Shark Bay, including the Rufous hare-wallaby.

FACT FILE

AUSTRALIA

Shark Bay's Bernier and Dorre islands protect a population of more than 4,000 Rufous hare-wallabies.

IUCN Red List status of Rufous hare-wallaby: vulnerable

Category:

Criteria:

The islands of Shark Bay have dry landscapes, covered in grasses and shrubs, which provide food for the vulnerable Rufous hare-wallabies.

grasses

Rufous hare-wallaby

dry land

TIMELINE

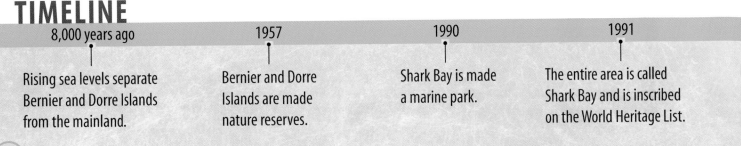

8,000 years ago
Rising sea levels separate Bernier and Dorre Islands from the mainland.

1957
Bernier and Dorre Islands are made nature reserves.

1990
Shark Bay is made a marine park.

1991
The entire area is called Shark Bay and is inscribed on the World Heritage List.

20

Important Features

The Rufous hare-wallaby is about the same size as a rabbit. It is a **marsupial**, so the females keep their young in a pouch where they feed and protect them. Rufous hare-wallabies are **nocturnal,** coming out of their burrows at night to feed.

Issues

The Rufous hare-wallaby was once found in many desert areas of Australia, but rabbits and other **introduced species** destroyed their natural habitat. Foxes and cats prey on Rufous hare-wallabies. This is part of the reason why the species no longer exists on the Australian mainland. It is vital to make sure that these introduced predators do not get onto Bernier and Dorre islands.

These shrubs and grasses provide shelter and food for the Rufous hare-wallabies. They are undisturbed by introduced species on the islands.

GLOSSARY

sea grass	grass-like plants that grow in the sea
marsupial	a kind of mammal that carries its young in a pouch
nocturnal	active at night
introduced species	plants or animals that are not native to an area

Sichuan Giant Panda Sanctuaries — Wolong, Mt Siguniang, and Jiajin Mountains

FACT FILE

CHINA

Sichuan Giant Panda Sanctuaries protects 500 of the 1,600 giant pandas still living in the wild.

IUCN Red List status of giant panda: endangered

Category:

Criteria:

Endangered giant pandas of the Sichuan Giant Panda Sanctuaries feed on up to 60 types of bamboo plant but they prefer some types more than others.

Sichuan Giant Panda Sanctuaries is made up of seven nature reserves and nine parks, all connected, as a place for protecting giant pandas. An **alpine** area of forests and grasslands, it is the largest and most important remaining habitat for the giant panda.

giant panda

forest with bamboo

TIMELINE

1949–60s	1963	1990s	2006
Human population growth reduces the panda habitat and pandas are hunted for food.	Wolong Giant Panda Nature Reserve is established to save the pandas.	Laws are introduced, controlling gun use and human access to the reserves, to protect the pandas.	The site is inscribed on the World Heritage List.

Important Features

Pandas mostly live at high **altitudes**. From autumn to spring, pandas live below 9,190 feet (2,800 meters), feeding on umbrella bamboo. In the summer, pandas move further up to cooler forests of **conifers**, where they feed on arrow bamboo.

Issues

The growing population of people around the sanctuaries is threatening the pandas. Pandas need to be able to move from area to area, but their habitat is fragmented by human activities, such as logging and farming. One alternative would be for local people to train as guides to the World Heritage area or as **conservationists**.

Conservationists look after baby or orphaned pandas found in the area. Pandas are very popular in China, so they are looked after well despite the threats to their habitat.

Did You Know?

The panda is the symbol of the World Wildlife Fund.

GLOSSARY

alpine	of high mountains
altitudes	heights above sea level
conifers	trees or shrubs like pine trees that grow seeds on cones
conservationists	people who protect an area

The Sundarbans/ Sundarbans National Park

The Sundarbans is an area on the border of India and Bangladesh. It is where the rivers Ganges, Brahmaputra, and Meghna break up into about 400 different streams of water as they enter the Indian Ocean. The Sundarbans includes the largest **mangroves** in the world, and it protects a number of endangered species, including the Ganges River dolphin.

FACT FILE

The Brahmaputra river system of the Sundarbans protects about 264 Ganges River dolphins.

IUCN Red List status of Ganges River dolphin: endangered

Category:

Criteria:

Endangered Ganges River dolphins live in the World Heritage sites of the Sundarbans and further up the rivers.

Ganges River dolphin

river

TIMELINE

1875	1977	1987	1997
Part of the Sundarbans area in India is made a forest reserve.	Bangladesh makes its Sundarbans area a wildlife sanctuary.	Sundarbans National Park, India, is inscribed on the World Heritage List.	The Sundarbans, Bangladesh, is inscribed on the World Heritage List.

Important Features

Ganges River dolphins cannot live in salty water. The area in which they can move about increases each year when heavy rains flood parts of the Sundarbans. The dolphins can then move into new areas in search of food.

Issues

Dams have been built on the rivers, **fragmenting** the dolphins' habitat. Farmers also use the rivers to water their crops, reducing the amount of water in the river system. This means that salty sea water has moved about 100 miles (160 kilometers) further into the river systems, preventing the dolphins from living there.

Did You Know?
The rivers are very dark and cloudy, so the dolphins send out high-pitched noises and listen to how they bounce back. By listening to the echoes, they can locate their prey.

The Sundarbans are surrounded by one of the densest populations of humans on Earth. This makes it difficult for the dolphins to live there.

GLOSSARY

mangroves   areas of trees growing in salt water
fragmenting   breaking up

Tasmanian Wilderness

The Tasmanian Wilderness is an area of vast forests and **alpine** areas in Tasmania, Australia. The protected area takes up one fifth of the island and protects a number of endangered species, including the Tasmanian devil, a **marsupial** that is **endemic to** Tasmania.

FACT FILE

AUSTRALIA
Tasmania

The Tasmanian Wilderness protects the Tasmanian devil.

IUCN Red List status Tasmanian devil: endangered

Category:

Criteria:

forest area

Tasmanian devil

The endangered Tasmanian devil is the largest marsupial carnivore in the world.

TIMELINE

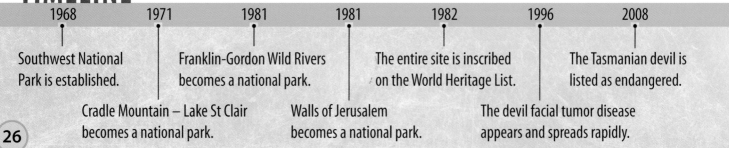

| 1968 | 1971 | 1981 | 1981 | 1982 | 1996 | 2008 |

1968 Southwest National Park is established.

1971 Cradle Mountain – Lake St Clair becomes a national park.

1981 Franklin-Gordon Wild Rivers becomes a national park.

1981 Walls of Jerusalem becomes a national park.

1982 The entire site is inscribed on the World Heritage List.

1996 The devil facial tumor disease appears and spreads rapidly.

2008 The Tasmanian devil is listed as endangered.

Important Features

Tasmanian devils are nocturnal **carnivores**. They prey on many animals, including birds, wallabies, and wombats. Since the 1990s, the devils have suffered from a type of cancer called devil facial tumor disease. This disease spreads rapidly and kills the devils after several months, because the tumors prevent them from eating.

Scientists check Tasmanian devils in the World Heritage site to monitor the spread of the devil facial tumor disease.

Issues

The devil facial tumor disease does not seem to have moved into much of the Tasmanian Wilderness. Scientists are not sure why this is, but they have sent unaffected devils from the Tasmanian Wilderness to different zoos to make sure the species does not get wiped out by this dreadful disease.

GLOSSARY

alpine	of high mountains
marsupial	a kind of mammal that carries its young in a pouch
endemic to	only found in
carnivores	animals that eat meat

Te Wahipounamu — South West New Zealand

Te Wahipounamu – South West New Zealand is an area of **fjords** and high cliffs running 280 miles (450 kilometers) along the southwest coast of New Zealand. The area protects a number of endangered and vulnerable species, including the Kea, an **alpine** parrot.

FACT FILE

NEW ZEALAND

★ South Island

Te Wahipounamu protects between 1,000 and 5,000 wild Kea.

IUCN Red List status of Kea: vulnerable

Category:

Criteria:

alpine grasslands

Kea

The vulnerable Kea of South West New Zealand is the only alpine parrot in the world.

TIMELINE

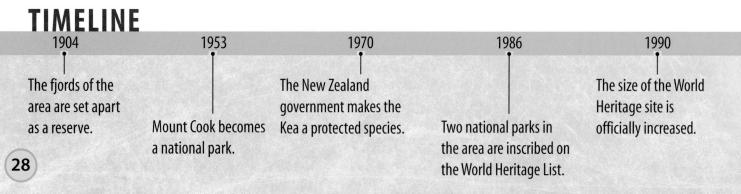

1904
The fjords of the area are set apart as a reserve.

1953
Mount Cook becomes a national park.

1970
The New Zealand government makes the Kea a protected species.

1986
Two national parks in the area are inscribed on the World Heritage List.

1990
The size of the World Heritage site is officially increased.

A mischievous Kea can pull the rubber off a car with its strong beak. Even though they can be pests the Kea are now protected because they are endangered.

Important Features

Kea live in a variety of habitats, including alpine areas and beech forests like those in Te Wahipounamu. They feed on insects, berries, and shoots, but in the past have also been known to attack sheep. Consequently, the New Zealand government offered a reward for killing them. About 150,000 were killed until the bird was given protection in 1970.

Issues

Stoats, cats, rats, and possums are moving into the Kea's habitat. These **introduced species** feed on Kea eggs. Poisoned bait is used to kill the introduced animals, but if a Kea eats the bait, it too will die. The park authorities are trying to create a bait that Kea will not eat.

Did You Know?
The Kea are very curious and intelligent. They can work together to solve problems like finding food.

GLOSSARY

fjords	narrow, deep inlets from the sea that flow between steep mountain sides or cliffs
alpine	of high mountains
introduced species	plants or animals that are not native to an area

Ujung Kulon National Park

Ujung Kulon National Park covers a peninsula and several islands off the south-west tip of Java, Indonesia. Half of the area is **rain forest**, while the other half is covered in other forest types, **mangroves**, and swamps. The park is home to many endangered species, including the Javan rhinoceros, one of the rarest large mammals on Earth.

FACT FILE

INDONESIA

Java

Ujung Kulon National Park protects between 40 and 60 Javan rhinoceroses.

IUCN Red List status of Javan rhinoceros: critically endangered

Category:

Criteria:

plants

Javan rhinoceros

thick understory of rain forest

The Javan rhinoceros is found in very few areas, including Ujung Kulon. It has one horn, unlike the African rhinoceros, which has two.

TIMELINE

1958
Ujung Kulon is made a nature reserve.

1967
Less than 30 Javan rhinoceroses are alive in the wild.

1991
The site is inscribed on the World Heritage List.

30

Important Features

The Javan rhinoceros used to live throughout Southeast Asia. However, it now only lives in two small places, the largest of which is Ujung Kulon National Park. The Javan rhinoceros is **solitary**. Each animal has its own territory. It avoids human presence and therefore it keeps within the thick **understory** of the rain forest. It feeds on plants and fruit that have fallen to the ground.

The rain forest of Ujung Kulon is very thick, providing the Javan rhinoceros with a lot of protection.

Issues

The main threat to the Javan rhinoceros comes from people killing it for its horn and other body parts to use in traditional medicine. **Poachers** continue to threaten the rhinoceros population, but park managers guard the park in order to protect the species.

Did You Know?
You cannot see a Javan rhinoceros in any zoo in the world. They are not held in any form of captivity.

GLOSSARY

rain forest	a forest that receives a lot of rain
mangroves	areas of trees growing in salt water
solitary	living alone
understory	area beneath the trees of a forest
poachers	people who hunt animals in an area where it is not allowed

Index